Learn Thesen Potteries Dialect

Barry Potter

Disappointing Publications

Contents

Let's get started!

Ayup	Y'alreet marrer?
Hello	*How are you, my friend?*
Ayup duck, ow at?	Wut dust knowst?
Hello, how are you?	*What's new?*
Adoo	At geen?
How do you do?	*How are you (going on)?*
Toe rate?	Arm orate, me owd
How are you?	*I'm very well, my friend*

Handy phrases

Familiarise yourself with these phrases. Read them aloud several times and try to memorise them.

Ayup duck, waste bin?
Hello, I haven't seen you lately, where have you been?

I've bin bad but arm orate nar, ta. Ow at?
I have been unwell but I am now recovered, thanks. And you?

Fang olt o' this duck
Would you mind holding on to this sir/madam?

Meet the family!

Cultural tip...

In formal situations, North Staffordshire people may greet each other with a firm handshake. You can address them with the friendly *marmate* or *marrer* (for men) or *duck* (for men or women). Do not greet them with a kiss on each cheek, unless you are very closely related, or you want to get *lamped*.

Marlady	*Girlfriend or fiancée*
Toad lady	*Wife or mother*
Owd mon	*Husband or father*
Feyther	*Father*
Maytherin-loower	*Mother-in-law*

Handy phrases

Me feyther's gone bookies
Father is the sporty type

The mayther-in-loower wants know Meg's Arse
My wife's mother is the inquisitive sort

Theyt a narky wench
You are a highly strung young woman

Marlady's got oller legs
Wy wife/girlfriend enjoys a drink

Toad Lady's got two brothers, one's got kids but tuther's gee

I have two brothers-in-law. one of them has children

Getting around!

At the bus stop

Dust goo Badly Grain?
Does this bus go to Baddeley Green?

Wut tarm dust lave?
What time do you leave?

Wee rat gooin? At gooin dine Castle?
Are you going to Newcastle?

No, soon lea gooey nup Anley
No, this bus only goes to Hanley

IS THIS THE RATE RUDE FER OATEN TYRES?

AR, BUT THEYT AFTER PED A LARDER DUCK OR THEEL AVE IT DARK

At the taxi rank

Armour chisit?
How much is the fare?

Ar conna affowd it, drop us at Eileen
I'm short of cash, drop me off at High Lane

Asking for directions

Cost shoe me the wee fer ...?
Can you show me the way to ...?

Theyt mart be reet if theyt turn rate, on tuther and, left mart be reet.
I bet you wish you'd bought a map

7

Going out!

The Potteries has many different types of eating places offering both local fare and a wide selection of international cusine. You can choose from **Curry ices**, **Char nays** or **Tar**, **Tally un** and **Farn darning**.

Handy phrases

Ate in or tacky tight?
Are you eating in or taking it away?

Rappy tup duck, arm gooin tacky twom
Wrap it up please I am taking it home

Cultural tip...

In North Staffordshire the pub is a place where people pop in for a drink and to informally chat and exchange views and ideas with their friends and neighbours. Some food may also be available, but the emphasis is on getting **ommered**.

Ard lark summer tate
I would like to see the menu please

Heg frayed race
Egg fried rice

Ommer nex
Ham and eggs

Arm clemmed
I am very hungry

Arm as full as a fat leedy's sock
No desert, thank you

In an emergency!

North Staffs folk take pride in the fact that they are known to be some of the friendliest people in the country.
However it is always useful to know at least a few basic medical phrases for use in an emergency.

Handy phrases

Weers thos spittle?
Which way is it to the hospital?

Ar brok meyip and eat rex, ar nade a woe kean stick
I have broken my hip and it very painful, I need a walking stick

Dunna fret, theyt soon be agate agin
Don't worry you will soon be on your feet again

Arv gorra favour / arm gooin dine with summit
I have a fever / I have a virus

Marlady as hearth raytis inner nay
My wife has an arthritic knee

Noss, when can ar rexpect mar hex ree?
Excuse me nurse, when am I to be X-rayed?

Pronunciation tip...

In the standard usage of Potteries dialect, aitches are dropped and randomly inserted before words beginning with vowels.

"Hour Highleen thinks ers rate posh since shay moved ter Haudley. "
"Huncle Arry hanna bayn sane a rind since ay bowt an and grenade off Hee-bay".

Arv gorra bun up, tanner budged fer thray wek
I am constipated

Anna bin rate free jees
I have been unwell for a while

Ar want goo wom
I would like to go home

Ast on the mend?
Are you feeling better?

Ay's Stoon Jed
He is deceased

ARM TOO POORLY FER GOO WOK ARV GORRA SPLIT NED EEK

DUNNA WERRIT SOON LEA A COWD

11

The North Staffordshire Duck

You may be surprised to hear North Staffordshire menfolk call each other 'duck'.

This is the *de facto* local term of endearment, transcending age, gender, sexual preference, class, race and even species.

Etymologically speaking, the origin of duck is not entirely clear. It could come from the Saxon word *ducas* which was a term of respect, and also where the word *Duke* arises from.

However duck could also relate to the Roman military title *Dux*, meaning troop or tribal leader. but it is not known if *ducas* pre-dates *Dux* or if the words are related. *Eat's a birruva miss tree duck.*

Cultural tip...

Potteries folk interchange 'learn' and 'teach'... so you can 'learn' yourself Potteries dialect, however you can also 'learn' it to someone else.

A similar confusion exists with 'lend' and 'borrow' (***borra***).

"Ayup, cost borra us a tenner?

"Orate, soo long us theyt lend it back."

Lets' talk about the weather!

A good opening gambit in any conversation is an exchange about the probability of *reen*. This may come in *shires* or it might *po dine* or *slat dine*. In winter it is advisable to *carry a numb brella reen or sharn*.

Eat's black ower Bill's mayther's [1]

It is going to rain

Eat's puthery

It's likely to rain

Eat's wet reen

It is drizzling persistently

[1] Neither Bill nor his mother have ever been satisfactorily identified, however this phrase is also common in Derbyshire, Nottinghamshire and the Black Country.

13

Are you ready for some more difficult phrases?

Ast shat the bed?
You are up earlier than usual

Arm stuck bay twayn a rock anna nard pleece
The wife and mother-in-law are conspiring against me

Ay wunna be wom til the gaise fly over
I expect he will be staying out late

Another crack lark that an theyt foe in it
Your attempt at humour has fallen flat

Pronunciation tip...

The Potteries vowel sound 'ow', as in cow, should always be used in place of 'ol' or 'oll', as in old (***owd***) or bold (***bowd***) or rolled (***rowd***)

Thee custna if thee wust, cust?
You wouldn't if you could, would you?

Shay conna trapper pig upper nen tree
She has bandy legs

Shonna shift shat
Stay where you are, don't move

Cost kick a bo agen a woe an yed it till it bosts? [2]
Can you kick a ball against a wall and head it back until it bursts?

Now theyt ow ready fer goo!

---

[2] This phrase is traditonally considered to be the ultimate test of correct Potteries dialect usage. However it is highly unlikely to crop in casual conversation and only ever appears in books about Potteries dialect.

Pronunciation tip...

Potteries people use na at the end of the word to make it a negative. eg. shall not becomes **shonna**, would not - **wudna**, can not- **conna** ... etc.

POTTERPEDIA

A

abayd *v.* tolerate, endure.

abite *adv.* similar to. *"Abite as much use as Anne Frank's drum kit".*

ackers *n.* money, cash.

agoo *adj.* in the past.

afe ender *n.* half a brick *"The mayther-in-loower were gerrin on me wick soo ar lamped er with afe ender".*

afower *prep.* previous to, ahead of. *"Ar wesh ard noon she ad er peas afower ar wen tight wither".*

agate *prep.* about, around. [From the Norse *gata*.] *"Anna sayn thee agate leetly, waste bin?" "Ar anna bin ite the ice, arv bin bad".*

ah rice *n.* where I live. *"Thee can say Mow Cop from ah rice".*

ailing *adj.* unwell. See also **bad.**

an ow *adv.* also, as well as.

angst *v.* an anxious wait. *"Ast got any bog roll in theer?" "Arl tell they if thee angst on a bit".*

Anley *n.* the largest of the Six Towns of Stoke-on-Trent. Birthplace of Arnold Bennett and Sir Stanley Matthews.

Anley opscotch *n.* the nimble footwork required to dodge puddles of sick while traversing the town centre on a Saturday night.

Anthea Turner *1 n.* Stoke born TV presenter and former consort of **Bruno Brookes.** *"Bay keer ful with that Flake duck, theyt do thesen a miss chafe".* *2 n.* rhyming slang for E's, ecstasy (Anthea Turners = gurners). "Garth you're talking utter bollocks again, have you been on the Antheas?" *(*Gabby Logan, BBC1 Final Score*).*

ar *adv.* yes.

ar tellst thee *v.* pay attention.

The novelist Arnold Bennett was born in Hanley in 1867. Although his most famous works drew inspiration from his early life in the Potteries, he left his home town at the earliest opportunity and was in no hurry to return. He compared the Potteries to Dante's vision of hell, which is something you won't find in the local tourist literature.

Bennett is the only celebrity from the Potteries to have a dish named after him. While the author was staying at the Savoy Hotel in London the chef made him an omelette with smoked haddock, Parmesan cheese and cream. Bennett liked it so much that he had it being prepared wherever he went. 'Omelette Arnold Bennett' has featured on the Savoy breakfast menu ever since, however you will notsee it on many menus *up Anley.* Much less fussy when it came to drink, Bennett died in 1931 of a terminal attack of *the squits* after downing a glass of typhus-infected tap water in a Paris bar.

Slightly interesting Potteries fact...

Present tense of *ar towd thee.*

ark *conj.* query. *"Toe rate ark?" "Ar, at they?'*

arrers *n.* the only sport in which you can participate while having a **paint.** The professional game is largely dominated by players from North Staffordshire *ie.* Phil 'The Power' Taylor, Ted 'the Count' Hankey and Adrian 'Jackpot' Lewis.

arse *adv.* denial. *"Did you traipse dogshit through the ice when you come in last nate." "Did I arse".*

arse crame *n.* a frozen diary product.

arsen, arsel *pro.* ourselves.

ast *v.* prelude to an enquiry. *"Astanyonyer?"* [3]

asard *adv.* next to. *"Theyt sit asard may lass then ar wunna fail the draft from the doower".*

assy dice *n.* 1990's dance music genre character-ised by electronic pulsing sounds, an extension of *ice music.*

at *v.* are you, abbreviation of 'art thou?' See also **wee rat.** *"At gooin ite ternate?" "No, arm skint so arm steen wom".*

author pay dick *n.* branch of medicine that deals with the prevention or correc-tion of injuries or disorders of the skeletal system and associated muscles, joints, and ligaments.

ayn sart *n.* a wonderful thing. *"Mar yed's bangin this moanin. With ayn sart ar would not ave necked that fiftaynth Jagerbomb."*

ayup *exclam.* informal greeting. *"Ayup, owat?" "Arv gorra touch of hearth raytis otherways ar conna com pleen".*

avergoo *v.* make an attempt. Encouragement to defend-er who crosses the half way line with the ball at his feet. *"Gooorn lad avergoo!"*

---

[3] I am looking to purchase some illegal substances and you look like the sort of chap who may be able to oblige me.

B

back rude *n.* toilet.

backend *n.* see **owtum**

backsies *n.* alleyways behind rows of **terry stices.**

bad *adj.* in poor health, ill. *"Marlady's bad in bed and woss up"..*

bains *n. what they ast on towst.*

bay leaf *n.* a kind of furniture remover.

baych *n.* where Potters go to soak up the sun.

bayer *n.* the fourth element after earth, wind and fire. You drink it in **paints.**

beck sard *n.* a posh arse.

belter *1 adj.* something very big or very good *2* a very attractive **wench.** *"Kinnell our youth, thar new snifter's a belter. Wheer dust farn dem?" "Shay threw up on me treeners in Spowns, ar said get thee cowt duck theyt pulled!"*

berry *v.* forecast. *"Berry tanner reened a tome. Owleys the seem when way goo awee nollerdee."*

Berryhill barbecue *n.* social gathering during which people drink cans of lager while standing around a burning Vauxhall Astra.

Biddle *n.* North Staffs town. According to folklore a number of families in the area, the *Biddle Turks*, are descended from slaves captured during the Crusades. The source of the River Trent is in nearby *Biddle Moower.*

black eye fraydee *n.* the last Friday night in **Castle** before **crimbo.**

blart *v.* to cry or sob uncontrollably, something a **mardarse** might do [from the Old English *blaten* - bleating of sheep.]

block furee scottoo *n.* posh cake serve in **farn darning** establishments.

Bombee *n.* one of the Potteries longest established **curry ices.** *"Put the budgie cover on, feyther's bin* *the Bombee".*

boon charna *n.* a type of pottery, as its name suggests, made from *boon*, usually *cow boon*, although in rare cases you could be eating off of a plate made from a person who is **jed.**

browt *v.* purchased. *"It's marlady's bothdee sewer browter summit from Pined land"*

bo *n.* spherical object which in the Tony Pulis tradition is kicked long or hurled into the penalty area from the touchline.

bob off *v.* play truant.

bonk *1 n.* hill. *2 n.* factory, as in **potbonk.**

Boslem *n.* the *mayther tine* of the Potteries. Home of Port Vale, birthplace of Josiah Wedgwood, **Lemmy** and darts champion Phil 'the Power' Taylor.

Boslem breakfast, full *n.* a shit followed by a cigarette.

bost *adj.* burst or **brock**.

bosted *adj.* hit by the ugly stick. *"Shay ad a feece lark*

a bosted mattris". See also **drinks under the darts bowered.**

bothdee *n.* anniversary of one's birth, special occasion on which to get **ommered.**

bottle kiln, bottle oven *n.* in the heyday of the local ceramics industry as many as 4,000 could be seen on the Potteries skyline with around 2,000 still standing in the 1950's. Only 47 remain, all listed buildings.

bowk *n.* t*heyt raydin wun reet nar lark, theers loods in lar bree. "Marlady's feveer reet is Fifty Sheeds Agree."*

brate *adj.* luminous, shining. *"Ow things brate an beowtiful / Ow cray chers greet an smow".*

brazzle *n.* hard or hard faced, as in *ard as brazzle*. Named after the iron pyrites nodules found in mines.

breen *n.* body part located in **yed.** Other body parts include *nay, elber, ip, backboon* etc.

Bri Nedge *n.* hilly village in

Potteries dialect is the closest of all English dialects to Anglo-Saxon Old English. Many of the words used in North Staffordshire today are the sole remaining vestiges of a language now extinct.

It is said that if you try to read the 14th century poem *Sir Gawain and the Green Knight* in a Potteries accent it suddenly makes perfect sense.

So, a broad Potteries accent might be an obstacle to professional success and damage your chances of upward social mobility, but on the upside it will come in very handy when you are reading obscure medieval alliterative poetry.

Slightly interesting Potteries fact...

the northernmost part of Staffordshire where urban legend has it everyone is related. *"They keep thesells to thesells up theer, if thee knowst worra mayn"*.

brine doff *adj.* disconsolate, fed up. *"Arm brine doff, thee anna gorenny brine sowce"*.

brock *1 adj.* broke, broken. *2 adj.* skint. *"Arm brock 'cos someone brock in me ice and pinched me things."*

brode bond *n.* the most efficient way to **dineLood** porn from *thin ternet*.

brung *v.* brought. *"Ar anner brung me omework, it's bin heaten bar the dog"*.

Bruno Brookes *n.* Potteries born Hobbit looky-likey who rose to prominence in the 1980's as a Radio 1 DJ and Top of the Pops host. While presenting the Top 40 in 1992 Bruno unwittingly played the full uncensored version of *Killing in the Name* by Rage Against the Machine, including 17 'fucks', an all time record for daytime on-air expletives. He once told *Nuts* magazine that he has a tattoo of a pirate on his left thigh, acquired during the Radio 1 Roadshow tour as part of a bet with his producer, who in return drank a pint of vinegar. See also **Anthea Turner.**

bun, bun up *adj.* constipated.

buzz *n.* form of public transport not requiring a seatbelt. See **PMT.**

C

cack *n.* excrement [from the Norse *cakkin*]. *"When Wilko waam dup Thar Snull weer cackin thisells."*

cack anded *adj.* not dextrous.

cant *n.* a person who tells *teels* (use with caution south of Watford).

Castle *n.* Newcastle-under-Lyme, despite proximity to Stoke-on-Trent, not one of the Six Towns. *"Theyt mart goo Castle on a Fraydee*

Potteries dialect has a curious kinship with *Marked RP* - the ultra-posh variant of Received Pronunciation spoken *dine sithe* (*eg* by older members of the royal household).

The Queen pronounces town as *tine* and house as *hice*. In a BBC interview she once recalled that during the VE day celebrations she ran *rind* to the front of Buckingham Palace with her sister, where they both *shited*.

Her husband Prince Philip, doing his usual bit for public relations, once described the Potteries as "ghastly". He also described Tom Jones as "a bloody awful singer". So not a fan of *Delilah* then either.

Slightly interesting Potteries fact...

nate, but up Anley on Satdee nate".

Chaydle *n.* market town situated between Stoke-on-Trent and Leek, home of the *Chaydle Cowboys* and just *dine the rude* from **Oaten Tyres.**

chays *n.* dairy produce best eaten with **oatcakes** or on *towst.* *"Chays an oatcakes - para darse!"*

cheer *n.* support for one's *beck sard.*

choke *n.* ancient teaching accessory, used either as a missile or to write on a *blockbode.*

chonnuck *n.* turnip, an important ingredient in **lobby.**

chunter *v.* complain, grumble.

chops *1 n.* mouth, **gob** *2 n.* chatter, excessive talk. *"Tharlady's got moower chops sn than our butchers".*

cirtle *n.* elipse. *"Ast ever bin dine that Lundin lark? "Ar, but never agin marmate. Way went dine th'undergrind and got lost on Cirtle Larn."*

clee *n.* material used in the manufacture of pots.

clemmed *adj.* very hungry, starving [From a Norse word meaning 'piched' due to fasting or starvation]. "

clues n. apparel. *"Theyt better get some clues on bay fower thee mayther comes rind."*

cob *1 n.* a tantrum, a bad mood. *"ay's gorra cob on"* *2* a measure of perspiration *"arm sweatin cobs".*

codge *v.* make a temporary repair.

come keen *v.* sharp or stinging pain. *"Me fayther got run over by the Silverdeel buzz. Ay's orate nar lark but them number ninety-fowers come keen".*

Conger tun *n.* town on the the A34 trunk road between Stoke and Manchester, just beyond the northernmost limit of Potteries dialect.

conna *v.* can not.

coss *v.* to swear at or abuse.

cost *v.* can you. [abbreviation of the Shakespearian 'couldst thou'].

cowd *n.* handy excuse for missing **wok.** If you don't wear enough **clues** you might *ketch cowd* or it could even develop into *mon flu.*

crapper *n.* the place where you might experience a rectal revolt following a trip to the **curry ice.** *"Ard give the crapper ten minutes if ar were you, your holiness, marlady's adder dodgy prone vindaloo".*

crash *v.* distribute. *"Abite tarm theyt crashed thee fags".*

crine grain bools *n.* popular outdoor sport for the elderly.

crog *v.* to jump a queue or gain admission without paying. *"Ar much giraffe pee goo Trentum Gardins?" "Ar dunna noo, way owleys crog in."*

crimbo *n.* annual celebration of the birth of commercialism, the fiest public bank holiday before **black eye fraydee.**

Cultural Quarter *n.* doesn't have a **Spowns.**

curry ice *n.* generic name for restaurants specialising in food from the Indian sub-continent *eg.* The Bom bee, The Coo ee noower, The Monzle etc. See also **runner, doing a.**

cut *n.* canal.

cut up *adj.* sad, upset

D

Day rude *n.* the A500 in Stoke-on-Trent.

deckit *v.* desist, stop. See also **paki tin.**

dee *n.* opposite of **nate.**

deed *adj.* lifeless, expired. *"Theyt dead rate, that dog's as deed as a dower neel."* See also **Stoon Jed.**

deef *adj.* unable to hear.

derry licked *adj.* abandoned, run down. In the post-industrial era, large swathes of Stoke-on-Trent were *derry licked.*

dineloods *n.* stuff you get

from *thin ternet.* See also **brode bond.**

dinner *n.* mid-day meal between breakfast and tea.

disser lied *adj.* ruled out. *"Ow Stoke gooin on owd duck, asturd?" "Way adder gool disser lied. The cried went whaled".*

Doc true *n.* a *tarm load.*

doffer *v.* prelude to disappointment. *"Doffer bar thee a paint but arm skint".*

done a noah *v.* fail to recognise. *"Tinner mar babby. Ar done a noah from Adam".*

doofer *n.* a hand held device *eg* a TV remote control, *as in* any gadget that will *do fer…*

dowton fig rains *n.* locally produced pottery figures made from *po slean* or **boon charna.** At one time every home in North Staffs had at least one of these collectible items on their mantlepiece (*eg* Th'owd Bloon Seller). It was however er extremely rare for money to change hands for them, which may explain why the company who made them, Royal Dowton, went bust.

drined,   drineded   *adj.* drowned.

drinks under the darts bowered *euph.* descriptive of a lady who is not conventionally attractive, See also **bosted.**

drug up *adv.* raised, reared. *"Put wood in thole, waste drug up, in a failed?"* [4]

duck(s)   *n.*   transgendered Potteries greeting or term of endearment for male or female. *"Big Issue duck?" "No ta duck, ar dunner raid eat".*

dunna *v.* do not.

dun teat *v.* query, does it not.

dust *v.* query [abbreviation of 'doest thou'.] *"Dust fancy a paint?" "I could use one, mar throat is as drey as a larm burner's clog".* [5]

---

[4] Shut the door. Where were you raised, in a field?

The Potteries legend Sir Stanley Matthews played professional football at rhe highest level until he was fifty years old, only to regret later that he had retired too soon.

He played his last competitive game age seventy-three. A near-vegetarian teatotaller, he attributed his career longevity to a fanatical dedication to fitness.

STANLEY MATTHEWS, Blackpool's quicksilver outside-right, has been capped for England no less than 33 times. Stan takes his training very seriously and soon discovered the cigarette which suited him best. "It wasn't till I changed to Craven 'A,'" he says, "that I learnt what smooth smoking meant."

"The cigarette for me"
SAYS FOOTBALL GENIUS **STANLEY MATTHEWS**

EVERY WEEK crowds warm to the brilliant technical play of master-schemer Stan Matthews—football's greatest name to fans and players alike. Like so many leading sportsmen Stan's a Craven 'A' smoker. "For a really satisfying cigarette that's kind to your throat," he says, "give me a Craven 'A' every time."

P.S. *That cork tip really does make a difference, you know. There's a lot more pleasure in a cigarette with an end that's always clean, and dry, and firm between your lips*

CRAVEN 'A' *smooth,* <u>*clean*</u> *smoking*

E

Eapdeal *n.* park and museum based around former *cool marn.*

eat *pro.* it.

Edward Smith, Captain *n.* **Anley** born captain of the tragic HMS Titanic. *"Haceberg? Ar conna say no haceberg!"*

Eeds *n.* a dangerous sexually transmitted disease caused by the retrovirus *Each Harvey. "Ast gorrer cowd?" "It mart bay Eeds, ar didna weer a rubber".*

eileen *n.* **rude** connecting **Anley** with Chell.

entry *n.* alleyway between two **terry stices.**

essole *n.* before the advent of central heating, the bottom of a solid fuel fireplace.

ex *v.* ask, enquire. *"Wee rat?" "Ar dunner know. Way could start bay exin fer sum sahns ter be purrup".*

F

fail *v.* sensation of being. *"Ar dunner fail rate ar mart bay comin dine with Ay boola."*

far narts *n.* art created for it's own sake, rather than usefully, for example *poor tree.*

farn darning *n.* a style of eating not involving curry, apparently. Could however involve *prone cock teels* or possibly **block furee** scot-too.

fang *v.* catch or seize.

fate *n.* inevitable altercation following drink. *"Thee dunna wants pick a fate in the middle of Aldi, theel bay ow over the Sent Null tomorrer".*

feece bowk *n.* social networking service.

---

[5] My throat is as dry as a lime burner's clog. Many local expressions are a living link to the Potteries of the pits and pots. The clogs worn by lime pit burners would split because of the heat of the pit.

Fenton *n.* the town Arnold Bennett forgot, unsurprisingly. Birthplace of TV personality Frank Bough. Through the 1970's and 80's Frank was the face of the BBC as a top sports presenter and frontman for Nationwide, Holiday and Breakfast Time. Until he admitted he liked to wear women's lingerie and have cocaine-fuelled S&M parties with prostitutes. The work dried up a bit after that.

Fenton Ferrari *n.* battery powered scooter ridden by *folk who are tow owd or tow fat fer woke.*

fer *adv.* towards, in order to. *"Arm gooin up Anley fer goo bookies duck".*

feyther *n.* male parent.

firkle, firtle *v.* grope, *cop a fail.*

fizzog *n.* face, usually that of a miserable person. [Derived from physiognomy, the pseudoscience of determining character from facial features.] *"Er as a fizzog lark a bulldog lick-*

ing piss off a nettle".

flit *v.* to move house.

flob *n.* expectorant, **gob.**

fodder, fowd *n.* sustenance. See also **snap** and **graze.**

foe *v.* drop, descend.

foe goo swell *idiom* if conditions are favourable. *"Foe goo swell, the Vale will avoid relly gee shun".*

fost, foggy *adj.* first. *"Bags ar goo foggy".*

fower *exclam.* warning to fellow golfers.

fowt nate *n.* two **wicks.**

frine *n.* a Vale fan might wear one during a Stoke cup run.

frit *adj.* frightened.

froz, frozzen *adj.* very cold, frigid. See also **perished.**

fuck a duck *idiom 1* expression of surprise, anger or disappointment *"fuck a duck, arv missed me buzz" 2* sexual intercourse with a waterfowl.

funt *v.* past tense of find.

furry teels n. horror stories

for children. They usually begin with the words "*Wun sponner tarm lark*".

furriner *n.* *1* alien, not native *2* a service unofficially provided using one's employer's facilities - *doing a furriner.*

G

G. Hoover's wet nieces *n.* annoying Christian religious group who preach by knocking on your door. If you want to get rid of them quickly tell them you are *Coth lick*, that usually works.

Garth Crooks O.B.E. *n.* Potteries-born ex-professional footballer and BBC football pundit known for his actorly manner, heroic but lapsed attempts to lose his local accent and stunning insights on the professional game *eg* "That goal surprised most people, least of all myself". In his 'team of the week' Garth once included West Brom's James Morrison, noting: "this is a player (England manager) Roy Hodgson should now be taking a keen interest in." Morrison was an established Scottish international.

gawp *v.* to stare at someone for a long time, possibly in an intimidating manner.

gee *1 n.* In Indian cusine, a type of clarified butter using in curries *2 n.* a chap who might *goo Pink up Anley.*

geen *adj.* going, going on.

glue bull waam in *n.* gradual increase in the overall temperature of the earth's atmosphere, generally attributed to the **grey nicey fect** caused by increased levels of carbon dioxide, CFCs, and other pollutants.

gob *1 n.* face. *2 v.* phlegm. See also **flob.**

goo *v.* move, proceed.

goose pear *v.* self destruct, explode with cataclysmic consequences. "*If ar turn* *theateen off marlady goose pear".*

Grace *1 n.* shit musical featuring John Travolta *2 n.* epicentre of the Eurozone fiscal meltdown making it the ideal destination *goo fer chape ollidee.*

graunch *1 v.* chew *2 v.* to grind one's teeth.

graze *n.* food, usually fast food eaten on the hoof.

greevy *n.* liquid dressing made from animal fat accompanying food *eg bonger zun mosh.*

grey nicey fect *adj.* see **glue bull waam in.**

grind *1 n.* what you hit when you *foe dine 2 n.* where they play **nogger.**

gyp *n.* a measure of suffering *"Mar nay's givin may gyp".*

H

hate *n.* altitude, tallness.

hex ree *n. they mart nayd one*

if theyt brok thee leg.

hersen, hersell *pro.* herself.

hissen, hisell *pro.* himself.

I

impotent *adj.* significant, meaningful.

ite *adj.* opposite of in.

J

jiggered *adj.* exhausted, politer version of *bollacksed, shag dite.*

jed a*dj.* deceased.

K

Kale yowknee *n.* university near to **Castle.** In 1982 the elderly bipolar comedian *Spark Milly Gun* was cruelly sacked as ambassador for *Kale yow knee* students. for failing to write an article for the rag magazine.

kaylard *adj.* state of inebriation. *"I have no recollection of of running that red light, your worships, I was totally kaylard"*. See also **ommered.**

kaypum paled *idiom* be on the alert, be observant. Catchphrase of TV crimefighter Shaw Taylor (ITV series Police 5 1962-92)

kebob ice *n.* late night one-stop shop for antisocial behaviour.

keem *v.* to scowl or pull a face.

kape on the bricks *v.* mind how you go. [From stay on the pavement, don't get run over]

kecks *n.* men's *trisers. "Toad Lady put me kecks in a not wesh bar me steak"*.

kedge *v.* beg or borrow.

keggy handed *adj.* left handed.

ketch *v.* catch.

kidder *n.* young person or younger brother.

Kidsgrew *n.* former mining town, near the site of *Thaircastle Tunnel*, said to be haunted be the ghost of murdered woman Kidsgrew Boggart.

kilt *adj.* killed

Kinnell *1 n.* George Kinnell, stalwart of Tony Waddington's Stoke team in the 1960's. *2 exclam.* expression of amazement or frustration. "Kinnell Garth, are you watching the same game as the rest of us?" - Dan Walker, BBC 1 Football Focus)

Knee burrs *n.* Australian TV soap opera.

knowst *v.* know. [abbrviation of Shakesperian *knowest thou*].

L

laggy *adj.* opposite of **foggy.**

lamp *v.* hit, strike with force,

The author HG Wells once spent three months in the Potteries with friends while recovering from an illness. His brief stay made an impression.

In *War of the Worlds* he described the scene of utter desolation after the Martian invasion. Wells said: "it reminded me, more than anything else, of the Potteries at night."

Slightly interesting Potteries fact...

harder than a *slop*. See also **thrape.**

lark *1 conj.* frequently used in Potteries dialect at the end of a sentence for no apparent reason, lark. *2* similar to. *"I'm shakin lark a shittin dog".* [6]

larner *n.* referee's assistant.

late *n.* illumination. At **Crimbo** you *mart goo up Anley see lates switched on.*

Late wood n. residential area south of **Neck End.**

learn *v.* teach.

leed up *adj.* ill, possibly with a **cowd.**

Lemmy *1 n.* Lemmy Kilminster, warty frontman of rock band *Mo Tred.* *"Th'ownlee card thee nayd, theece of speeds, theece of speeds" 2 v.* loan, advance *"Lemmy a tenner til Fraydee wut?"*

lobby *n.* one of the three major food groups (see also **oatcakes** and **Rate spays**). A heavy stew containing meat, potatoes and other vegetables served with or without dumplings, according to taste, traditonally eaten as fortifying meal in cold weather. [Probably a local variant of 'lobscouse', a dish imported by Liverpudlian navvies during the construction of the Trent and Mersey Canal in the eighteenth century.]

lozzack *v.* to rest or recline in a lazy manner. *"Theyt done nowt but lozzack rind the ice ow dee".*

lugole *n.* ear.

lung *adj.* considerable duration in time. *"Weer did ar get this cough? Eat's a lung story".*

lurry *n.* heavy goods vehicle, also called a *waggin* as in *Waggin a Nosses.*

---

[6] I have a bad case of *delerium tremens* as a result of having consumed a surfeit of alcohol last night.

M

mack v. create, bring about.

mard, mardarse *1 n.* whiny or complaining *2 n.* spoilt, usually a child.

marrer, marmate *n.* friend.

marlady *n.* wife or girlfriend.

marn *pro.* belonging to me.

mashin, *v.* brewing a pot of tea.

mate *n.* something you might have in your **snap** possibly a filling in a **pace**. *"But not poke if theyt a Moslem, theyn dunner ate eat lark".*

maythered *adj.* bothered, hassled, a mild state of confusion when one's train of thought has been, er... *"If that's thee mayther maytherin', tell er arm ite".*

Meg's arse *n.* the oracle, what a nosey person seeks to discover. A person who seeks to get to the bottom of something wants to know *Meg's arse".*

Meir salad *n.* chips.

moanin *n. the wost tarm of the dee Mundee ter Fraydee. "Good moanin? "Ar conna say owt good abite eat".*

mop *n.* sketch or plan of a geographical location.

mop, put the Potteries on the *idiom* any local event deemed to be of huge national significance *eg* the opening of a Starbucks. Shortly after appearing in his final show at the Regent Theatre, 62 year old actor and former pop idol Adam Faith died of a heart attack while servicing his 22 year old girlfriend in the Moat House Hotel. (His last words were "Channel 5 is all shit, isn't it? Christ, the crap they put on there. It's a waste of space".) This event really *"put the Potteries on the mop".*

moower *adv.* in greater quantity. *"Er's sane mower pricks than Phil Teeler's dart bowered".*

mucker *n.* friend or acquaintance. [of unknown origin. [in Ireland a mucker is a person who shovels shit].

mullygrub *v.* assault.

munter *n.* a lady not blessed by the beauty fairy. So unattractive that she still looks **bosted** even when viewed through *bayer goggles*. *"I dunna think I'll bay saying er again, Cilla. She is a munter"*. See also **drinks under the darts bowered.**

N

na *adv.* not. *"Conna, dunna, shonna, wunna"*.

nar *adv.* at the present time. *"Nar's the tarm fer ow gud men come ter theed of party"*.

narky *adj.* easily upset, quick to fly off the handle.

narnin cheese *n.* approx. diameter of an **oatcake.**

nate *n.* late evening, when you might *cow it a dee* and *goo up the wood nills*.

neck *v.* quaff, drink quickly

as in *"neck eat dine, eat's thar shite"*.

Neck End *n.* Longton, southernmost of the Six Towns, known locally as the *Neck End* of the city.

nesh *adj. term* used to describe a person who complains a lot about the cold [from the Old English *nesc* meaning tender] *"Ay's as nesh as a carrot"*. Often followed by the term 'Southern Jessie'.

noddle *n.* brain. *"Theyt mart use thee noddle afower opening thee gob"*.[7]

nogger *n.* football.

nollerdee *n.* a break from work or studies.

noss *n. 1* person trained in the care of the sick or infirm. The *Noower's Ark* in *Art Sill* was said to be handily placed if you wanted to pick up a *noss*. *2 n.* large hoofed mammal used for riding or racing. *"A noss, a noss, mar kin dum fer a noss"* (Richard III)

nova coot *n.* if you are **nesh**

---

[7] Engage brain before speaking.

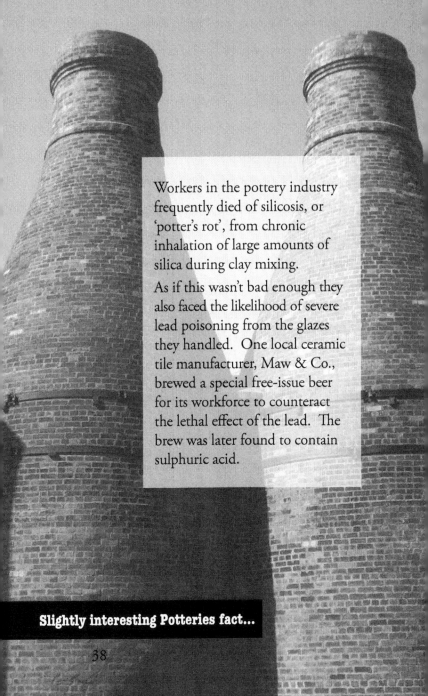

Workers in the pottery industry frequently died of silicosis, or 'potter's rot', from chronic inhalation of large amounts of silica during clay mixing.

As if this wasn't bad enough they also faced the likelihood of severe lead poisoning from the glazes they handled. One local ceramic tile manufacturer, Maw & Co., brewed a special free-issue beer for its workforce to counteract the lethal effect of the lead. The brew was later found to contain sulphuric acid.

Slightly interesting Potteries fact...

you will need one of these if you *goo Bree Tanya steedyum* (a difficult place to go to - copyright Gary Linekar, Gary Neville, Alan Shearer, Mark Lawrenson, etc.)

O

O *n.* historic building *eg Fode Grain O, Little Mowton O, Whitmoower O, Barley stun O.*

oatcake *n.* food of the gods. A type of pancake made from oatmeal, whole wheat flour, yeast, milk and water and cooked on a griddle. Potteries oatcakes were traditionally sold direct from the window of a house to customers on the street but the last producer in this style closed in 2012. Oatcakes can be eaten with all types of fillings but purists only eat them with **chays** and/or bacon. Origins of the North Staffs oatcake are uncertain: according to popular myth the oatcake has links with British colonial rule in India. Some claim that North Staffs soldiers took a liking to poppadoms and tried to copy them on their return to Staffordshire, but historical evidence dates the oatcake much earlier.

Oaten Tyres *n.* popular theme park near to the Potteries. *"If theyt gooin on the raids mek sure thee tek a cheen joe trisers."*

ockered *adj.* difficult, troublesome.

off sard *1 adj.* unwell, suffering from range of ilnesses from a **cowd** to near death. See also **leed up.** *2 adj.* an illegal move in football.

ommered *adj.* state of advanced befuddlement caused by prolonged use of alcohol.

Ommerend *n.* village in borough of Newcastle-under-Lyme near to *Ow Seejer's Bonk.*

ont piss *1 adj.* technical term for off centre. *2 adj.* out with the lads/ladies drinking **paints**.

39

North Staffordshire's Titanic Brewery celebrates the local connection to Hanley-born Edward J. Smith, captain of RMS Titanic during the most infamous peacetime maritime disaster in history.

The brewery successfully exploits the unique marketing opportunity presented by the deaths of 1,517 men, women and children by drowning and hypothermia, with several disaster-themed pubs, offering a range of ales including Titanic Mild, Steerage, Iceberg, White Star and Captain Smith's Strong Ale. Cheers!

Slightly interesting Potteries fact...

onny rood *adv.* anyway, whatever.

oppy tart *n.* hunger, desire for food. *"Dunno way, arv got no oppy tart theys dees fer block furee scottoo."*

orate *1 adv.* alright, OK. *2* the No. 1 Potteries chat-up line, *"Orate?"*

owd *1 adj.* advanced in years *2 n.* friend. *"Orate me owd?"* See also **marrer, marmate.**

owleys *adv.* every time, on every occasion. *"shit appens but why does eat owleys appen to may?"*

owt *pro.* anything. *"In olden dess a glimpse of stocking / was looked on as something shocking / now heaven knows, / owt goos"* (Cole Porter, *Owt Goos*)

Owtum n. start of the football season. Also known as **backend.**

P

pace *1 n.* sandwich. *2 n.* state of mutual harmony *"give pace a chance".*

paint *n.* standard measure of liquid. *"Pull us another paint landlord, this un's flat as a kipper's dick".*

paki tin *v.* desist. See also **deck it.** *"Ar after stand ite sard in frayzin cowd fer av a fag but ar conna packy tin".*

pee dee *n.* the highlight of the month for a working Potter.

peggin *adj.* desperate. *"Arm peggin ferrer fag lark".*

Penkle *n.* hilltop township near Stoke with delusions of royal grandeur. *"Locals cow it a village burry tanner gorenny faileds rind it".* The actor Neil Morissey went *Penk Looms* and Sir Oliver Lodge, inventor of the spark plug, lived here. *"If thee spark plug's damp run yer motor dine Penkle bonk gerrit gooin agin".*

perished *adj.* very cold, when *mower* **clues** are required.

Pined land *n.* bargain shop. *"It's soo posh in Trentum thar've got a Farv Pined land".*

plea *v.* after school activity. *"Can Robbie come plea?"* *"No Jason, ay anna finished raytin ay's lireex".*

PMT *n.* former local **buzz** operator. *"Thee cowed it the PMT cos ketchin theer buzzes were such a stressful expayrience".*

po dine *v.* rain heavily, polite version of *pissin dine.*

Po till *n.* suburb of *Castle* where the *Potters whale* is.

pobs *n.* a mixture of bread and warm milk. *"Th'owd mon's bayn eighteen pobs ever since ay addis staith nock tite in a fate".*

poke *n.* the flesh of a pig.

potbonk *n.* a place where pottery is made.

potter's rot *n.* silicosis (see page 38).

pub crow *n.* spirited attempt

to get **ommered** by visiting as many pubs as possible in one drinking session.

puddled *adj.* stupid, mad, *"a few sarnies showt of a picnic".*

puthery *adj.* heavy or humid weather, *eg* when a thunderstorm is brewing.

Q

quate *adv.* quite

Quayns, the *n.* night club once famous for themed social evenings for singles, *eg* Thursday night usec to be *grab-a-granny* but later became a venue for disabled singles i.e. *powk-a-paraplaygic.*

R

rammel *n.* a rough looking dog, non-pedigree.

Rate spays *n.* locally manufactured baked pies.

real wee *n.* North Staffs had a network of these known as 'the Knotty' until the Beeching Cuts of the 1960's.

rind *adj.* the circle of life. *"what goos rind comes rind".*

ronk *adj.* a badass smell, like a reek but much worse. *"Thee feyther's fate ronk summer toe full".*

rot *n.* rodent of the genus rattus. *"Theers a rot in me kitch ean worramagonnadow?* (UB40)

rude *n.* way or highway. *"Ow rudes laid to Room".*

runner, doing a *v.* healthy alternative to paying the bill at the end of a meal in a **curry ice.** Unless it was *The Monzle* and they made you pay before you ate.

rumpty fizz *n.* archaic term descriptive of a *mucky leedy*, a politer version of *slapper* or *oower*.

S

sailing *n.* overhead interior, upper limit. *"Theyt look jiggered". "Ar am, ar spent ow dee har texing the sailing".*

safty *n.* this afternoon.

sate *n.* spectacle.

say *v.* look at, perceive, *dust say?*

scag off, crog off *v.* play truant.

scran *n.* food. See also **graze, snap.**

scrawp *v.* to nag or complain.

scummy night *n.* public acknowledgment of one's homosexuality. *"Trevor says ay's gee. Scummy night".*

seck nafe *n.* after half time. *"Did say Stoke awee on telly?" "Ar cowt seck nafe in Staffer Larf".*

seggy, segs *adj.* next in order of preference after **fogs** or **foggy.**

Sell a red *n.* crossroads at the junction of the A52 and

The fading of the farv thighs and

A520, location of the *O Per Nanker*.

sem tree *n.* where you go when you're **Stoon Jed.**

sen *n.* self.

Sentinelle *n.* section of the local evening newspaper set aside for the entertainment of ladies *eg* the *Sentinelle* makeover in which a random **munter** is transformed into a **belter** by providing her with a toothbrush and £10 in TopShop vouchers.

sennatucked *adj.* stiffness, possibly after sitting for too long or from bloating after a large meal. "*After eighteen fower chickin fur Rita's, ar was proper sennatucked*".

sew reet fer sum *idiom* the response to somone else's good news *eg* if you said to an American "I've had a new car" the reply might be "ossom" however the correct response in North Staffs is "*Sew reet fer sum*".

sgoowin *idiom* meteorological term. As in "*sgoowin reen, sgoowin snoo*".

shape *n.* ruminant mammals of the genus Ovis of the family Bovidae. Closely related to *gouts*.

shat *v.* shall you, will you. "*Thee shonna shift, shat?*"

sheed *v.* spill or lose. "*Lurry sheeds lood*" (Cheadle & Tean Times headline. See **Stunner**).

shite *1 n.* yell, exclamation - "*way are in extra tarm, eat's ow over bar the shiting 2 n.* call, prediction. "*Good shite!*" *3 v.* act of buying a round of drinks. "*Is it mar shite*". "*No, burrer left me wally tin tuther trisers, soo can you shite me up a painter Bass*".

shonna *v.* shall not. "*Shonna bay lung, back in a whale*".

shug *n.* term of affection, the sweet alternative to **duck.**

shoe *v.* demonstrate, show.

sick stain *n.* the legal age of consent.

signed *1 n.* noise or auditory effect. "*Ar dunner lark the signed of that cough. Get thesen sarned on*". *2 adj.* in good condition, healthy.

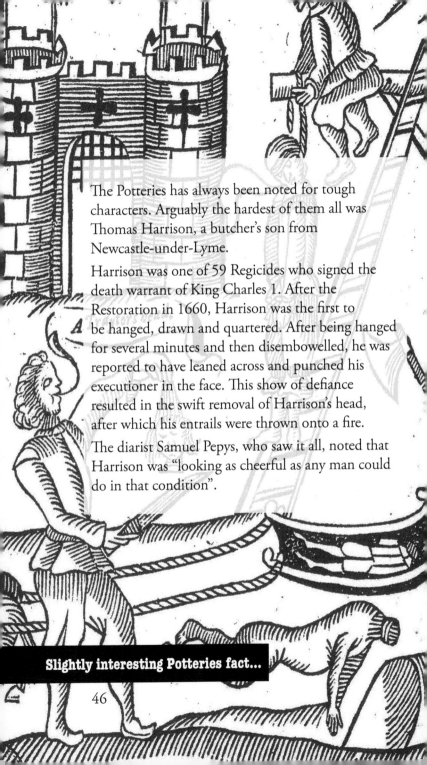

The Potteries has always been noted for tough characters. Arguably the hardest of them all was Thomas Harrison, a butcher's son from Newcastle-under-Lyme.

Harrison was one of 59 Regicides who signed the death warrant of King Charles 1. After the Restoration in 1660, Harrison was the first to be hanged, drawn and quartered. After being hanged for several minutes and then disembowelled, he was reported to have leaned across and punched his executioner in the face. This show of defiance resulted in the swift removal of Harrison's head, after which his entrails were thrown onto a fire.

The diarist Samuel Pepys, who saw it all, noted that Harrison was "looking as cheerful as any man could do in that condition".

Slightly interesting Potteries fact...

"Ar dunner lark the signed of that cough". "Dunner werrit, arm signed as a pined".

skoo *n.* place of education.

slar drool *n.* before the advent of calculators, an instrument used in a **skoo** for discovering *Kew Brutes* and other such mathematical problems.

slosh *1 v.* urinate. *"thee used ter frays yer conkers off in winter when theyt bin fur slosh."* *2 n.* stage alias of Saul Hudson, Potteries born guitar-botherer, most notably with Guns n' Roses.

slat *v.* to throw or chuck [From the Old English *slath.*] *"Eights slattin it dine".* See also **po dine.**

Smo thown rind a bite *n.* busy traffic juntion on *Eileen,* miracle of engineering, the modern Stonehenge.

snap, snappin *n.* lunch, usually packed to be eaten at **wok.**

snap bag, snappin wrappin *n.* lunch container.

sneep *n.* to snub or upset.

snifter *n.* girlfriend.

snot *v.* it is not, as in, *"snot gooin a wee ast put sum crame on eat?"*

snotty *adj.* bad tempered.

sowt *n.* seasoning for **Meir salad.**

spanwanned *adj.* the painful state of being stuck astride a **woe** whilst attempting to climb over it. [From the Anglo-Saxon *spannan winnan*].

Speen *n.* continental holiday destination *"the reen in Speen fows meenly on the Potters fowt nate".*

split ned eek *idiom* a continual sensation of pain in **yed.**

spom *1 n.* canned meat *2 n.* unsolicited emails, usually ofering penile extensions.

spon new *adj.* not acquired from a charity shop, *a pone browkers* or *secky nand off Hee-Bay.*

sprites *n.* one of your *farv a dee.*

squits *1 n.* diarrhoea *2 adj* even. *"Ar givim a bostlip*

47

and ay lamped me rind lugole, sewer squits".

stiff *adj.* fat, obese. A person overly fond of **Rate spays** and **Meir salad.**

Stoon Jed *adj.* lifeless person, possibly from small market town off the southbound A34.

strait *n.* public thoroughfare.

stripper *1 n.* in the manufacture of pottery, a girl who removes dry ware from the mould *2. n.* a person, who removes his or her **clues** for entertainment purposes.

strug n. something strange, anomalous, out of place, the **Cultural Quarter.**

Stunner *n.* nickname of North Staffs weekly newspaper *The Cheadle and Tean Times,* allegedly so called because its only useful purpose is for rolling up and swatting flies.

suck the mop *v.* put up with a bad situation because there is no viable alternative. "With no money to strengthen the squad and

the pitiful lack of talent available we just have to *suck the mop"* (Port Vale supporter, *Praise and Grumble Talkboard*).

summit *n.* an unspecified thing. If a thing is amiss, *summit's up.*

surry *n.* friend. [From the obsolete form of address for a man or boy *sirrah.*]

sut *v.* past tense of sit.

T

Tarms Queer *n.* in Longton, location of the *Cry No Tell.*

tarminate *adj.* after 9pm. *"Oo the yell is that at this tarminate?"*

tate *adj.* ungenerous, frugal. *"Thee brother's as tate as a duck's arse."*

tea *n.* the main meal of the day, eaten in the evening.

tea bull *n.* a place where posh people eat **snap** with *nar fun folk* while sat on **cheers.**

Terry stices *n.* linked dwelling in a row or terrace.

thar, tharn *pro.* your, yours. Sometimes **yorn.**

thee, they, theyt *pro.* you, you are.

thee assner ast? *exclam.* rhetorical question. *"Arv shot marlady deed". "Thee assner ast?"*

thesen, thesell *pro.* yourself, themseves. It was once possible to identify which part of North Staffordshire a person lived in by their dialect. *Thesen* is a Moorlands word and *thesell* is Potteries.

th'owd mon *n.* father, or husband of **Toad Lady**.

thrape *v.* strike, deal a blow. *"Dunna thrape thee sister soo ard, er anner finished weshing the crocks".* See also **lamp.**

thowt *n.* mental activity, *fowd fer thowt.*

thighs and *n.* standard minimum unit of weekly pay for professional footballers.

ticky tights *n.* you might meet them hanging out *dine Wembley Wee.*

tine *n.* on Tyneside it is called a toon *eg* Stafford is the *kinety tine of Staffy cher.*

tinna *adv.* it is not.

Toad Lady *n.* Potteries matriarch. *"Ast gooin the match?" "Ae dunno, arl after ex Toad Lady".*

toe *1 adj.* above average height. *2 adj.* difficult to believe. *"thee mayther tells toe teels".*

toe rate? *adj.* how are you?

toerag *1 n.* a worthless or useless person. [Possibly Irish origin] *2 n.* another name for an **oatcake.**

towd *v.* explained. *"What dust see to a woman with two black eyes?" "Nowt, theyt ow ready towd er twarce."*

Towk *1 v.* converse, communicate. *2 n.* village in the borough of Newcastle-under-Lyme, birthplace of Reginald Mitchell, aeronautical engineer and creator of the Spitfire.

towk brode *v.* speak with

a strong Potteries dialect. Like many local dialects there are subtle differences in speech across the region and it is said that the dialect was broader in **Tunster** and less pronounced in **Neck End.** The very broadest form is said to be spoken in *Biddle Moower.* "*Way gorra do summit abite eat afower eat dars ite ow tergether.*"

tra a bit *idiom* goodbye for now, see you later.

tripe *n.* was once traditional Potter's **snap.** Take the stomach lining of an ox, then wash and rinse. Soak the rinsed tripe in white vinegar for at least eight hours. Drain, rinse in cold water, cook for further two hours. Then throw it in the bin.

Tunster *n.* one of the Six Towns of Stoke on Trent, birthplace of Robbie Williams and Clarice Cliff, ceramic artist. Former home of the Northern Soul *The Toche,* famous for its *ow naters.*

Tunster tan *adj.* the reddish skin tone achieved by

gentleman who spend the day drinking cans of high strength lager al fresco.

U

upper tate *n.* early morning call. *"At gooin wok ter morrer?* "*Ar am, so knock may upper tate"*

Utcheter *n.* racy market town. According to folklore the most exciting thing that ever happened in *Utcheter* was when the famous lexicographer Samuel Johnson stood outside one day in the rain. Without a hat.

W

waste bin? *adv.* enquiry about one's movements. See also **wee rat?**

waiter *n.* liquid used in a **wesh.** A cheap beverage *"Excuse may weeter, ard lark* *some waiter".*

wee rat *adv.* enquiry about one's whereabouts. *"Wee rat bin?" "Arv bin poorly bad with me bladder soo ar anner bin ite".*

wench *n.* girl or young woman [Old English].

werrit *v.* concern, worry. *"Is it summit werrit abart?" "Dunner werrit thee sen, they tull bay orate"*

wesh *v.* ablution, cleansing action.

West pote leak *1 n.* A nature reserve, the largest body of water in the City. An exciting new adventure play area opened in 2006, with a range of modern play equipment. (SOT Tourist Information Centre) *2 n.* the City's premier dogging hotspot. *"The otter is one of our most majestic freshwater.... Christ on a bike, look at the norgs on that!".* (Ray Mears, Wild Britain ITV1).

Wheels *n.* holiday destination, source of daffodils, rugby and jokes about **shape.**

52

Whitmower *n.* posh accident blackspot, location of *Monry Narms.*

whaled *adj.* untamed, angry. *Theers whaled waller bays up the Roe Cheese.*

widder *n.* a woman who has lost her husband. eg. an **arrers** *widder. "Th'owd mon spends soo much tarm in pub ay mart as well bay deed."*

Wispa lean *n.* in Butterton, home of North Staffordshire Sports Club and a dump for used tyres.

wick *n. seven dees mack a wick - Mundee, Chewsdee, Wensdee, Thosdee, etc.*

woe *n.* wall.

wog *v.* steal.

wok *n.* employment.

woke *v.* form of exercise. *"Arv bin fer woke up Anley". "What fower, was thee no buzz"?*

woke awee *v.* turn the other cheek: *"leave it Rupert, woke awee, ay inner woth eat".*

wom *n.* a Potter's *wom* is his castle. See also **ah rice.**

Wooer *n. 1* armed fighting,

eg Fost Wowd Wooer, Fowk Lunds Wooer 2 village near *Parp Geet.*

woss *adj.* worse or worst, as in "*Theers nowt woss un tekkin a dump an farn dean theer's no bog roll left*" or "*Theers one thing woss than bayin towked abite, an that's not bayn towked abite*" (Oscar Wilde).

Wrekin gooin rind the *idiom* taking a circuitous route or not explaining something clearly. Named after a distinctive hill in nearby Shropshire. Also *Gooin Chaydle fer get Lake.*

Wrexham *v.* enquire about directions. "*Arm lost, ar laughter Wrexham the wee goo*".

wunna *v.* will not.

wut *1 v.* will you [abbreviation of 'wouldst thou'] *2 pro.* query, request for more information. "*Wut stunner bite?*"

XYZ

yawp *n.* loud annoying wail, usually by a small child in a supermarket.

yed *n.* at the football match mind you don't get *a boot rapt rind yours.*

yonks *adj.* a very long time. "*The dayner sewers deed ite yonks agoo*".

yorn *pro.* that which belongs to you. "*Sarned, sailed day livered, arm yorn*" (Stevie Wonder).

you'll ave it dark *idiom* get a move on, you're doing it too slowly.

youth, youther *n.* salutation, used mainly among males and regardless of age. "*Ayup youther, ast pick tup thee pension?*"

zif *conj.* like, similar to. "*Arm bartin me neels sif ar anner bin fed*".

Printed in Great Britain
by Amazon